Operation Catapult: The History of the Controversial British Campaign against the Vichy French Navy during World War II

By Charles River Editors

A picture of the French battleship *Strasbourg* under fire

About Charles River Editors

Charles River Editors provides superior editing and original writing services across the digital publishing industry, with the expertise to create digital content for publishers across a vast range of subject matter. In addition to providing original digital content for third party publishers, we also republish civilization's greatest literary works, bringing them to new generations of readers via ebooks.

Sign up here to receive updates about free books as we publish them, and visit Our Kindle Author Page to browse today's free promotions and our most recently published Kindle titles.

Introduction

A picture of British planes preparing for an attack against the Vichy French

Operation Catapult

"You are charged with one of the most difficult and disagreeable tasks that a British admiral has ever been faced with. But we have complete confidence in you and rely on you to carry it out relentlessly." – Prime Minister Winston Churchill

"90% of senior naval officers, including myself, thought [Operation Catapult] a ghastly error and still do." – Royal Navy Admiral Andrew Cunningham, 1950

Emerging from France's catastrophic 1940 defeat like a bedraggled and rather sinister phoenix, the French State – better known to history as "Vichy France" or the "Vichy Regime" after its spa-town capital – stands in history as a unique and bizarre creation of German Fuhrer Adolf Hitler's European conquests. A patchwork of paradoxes and contradictions, the Vichy Regime maintained a quasi-independent French nation for some time after the Third Reich invasion until the Germans decided to include it in their occupation zone.

Headed by a French war hero of World War I, Marshal Philippe Petain, and his later Prime Minister Pierre Laval, Vichy France displayed strong right-wing, conservative, and authoritarian tendencies. Nevertheless, it never lapsed fully into fascism until the Germans arrived to reduce its role to little more than a mask over their own dominion. Petain carried out several major initiatives in an effort to counteract the alleged "decadence" of modern life and to restore the strength and "virtues" of the French "race." Accordingly, he received willing support from more conservative elements of society, even some factions within the Catholic Church. Following Case Anton – the takeover of the unoccupied area by the Germans – native French fascist elements also emerged.

While the French later disowned the Vichy government with considerable vehemence, evidence such as fairly broad-based popular support prior to Case Anton suggests a somewhat different story. The Petain government expressed one facet of French culture and thought. Its conservative, imperialistic nature did not represent the widespread love of "liberty, fraternity, and equality" also deeply ingrained in French thinking, but neither did it constitute a complete divergence from a national history that produced such famous authoritarians as Louis XIV and Napoleon Bonaparte.

Of course, this precarious position left Britain in the unenviable position of figuring out what to do with its once erstwhile ally. France is seldom deemed a maritime power, yet during World War I and in the interwar period, the French Navy developed into a relatively powerful fighting force. While it could not rival the British, American, or Japanese forces, it represented one of the medium-sized naval powers like Germany or Italy. As such, the French Navy would have an interesting role to play in the development of the Vichy state during World War II.

When the Germans conquered northern France and forced the French to sign an armistice, the French fleet passed under the control of Vichy and its leader, Petain. Another key figure in the events surrounding the fate of the French fleet would be Admiral Francois Darlan, a complex man with both patriotic and ruthless elements who would ultimately die under strange and suspicious circumstances to an assassin's bullets.

While the Third Reich naturally cast covetous eyes at the powerful French naval vessels in the hands of their ostensible Vichy ally, they proved content to see those ships remain neutral for several years after their victory in Western Europe. Only when the French changed their allegiance in the direction of the Allies did the Germans make an attempt to seize the French vessels.

British Prime Minister Winston Churchill was not so content. The actions he initiated - opposed by many of the British naval officers involved, but nevertheless dutifully carried out - embittered relations between France and England for a generation. The stern leader showed a certain ruthlessness and even spitefulness in dealing with both neutrals and weaker allies during the war. England failed to provide material aid to Poland when the Germans and Soviets invaded it in 1939, and even neglected to declare war on the USSR. Churchill sacrificed Poland to Stalin's territorial ambition almost without a murmur of protest at war's end, and his successor, Clement Attlee, then carried on his existing policies by insisting the Poles pay a large sum to the Britain for British assistance, despite the fact that hundreds of thousands of Polish soldiers fought for the British only to see their homeland given away almost casually by their allies.

This somewhat unflattering side of Churchill's character emerged in his dealings with Vichy as well. Despite the assurances of Darlan and others that the French would never hand their ships over to Germany, Churchill would put in motion a campaign attempting to destroy their fleet. As a result, the one-sided Operation Catapult unfolded on the French Algerian coast in July 1940, and it would be one of the most controversial and unique episodes of World War II. It would also pit French and British forces against each other for the first time since the end of Napoleon's reign in 1815.

Operation Catapult: The History of the Controversial British Campaign against the Vichy French Navy during World War II looks at how the attacks unfolded. Along with pictures of important people, places, and events, you will learn about Operation Catapult like never before.

Operation Catapult: The History of the Controversial British Campaign against the Vichy French Navy during World War II

About Charles River Editors

Introduction

The French Fleet Before the War

The Establishment of Vichy France

The Vichy Fleet

The Start of Operation Catapult

Fruitless Negotiations

The Attack

The Aftermath of Mers-el-Kebir

Online Resources

Bibliography

Free Books by Charles River Editors

Discounted Books by Charles River Editors

The French Fleet Before the War

Like most of the countries that ill-advisedly participated in World War I, France emerged from the conflict in a dire economic condition. Although the French probably hoped that reparations from Germany would help to boost the national coffers and recoup the struggle's vast expense, Germany proved too depleted to make timely payments. The victors had claimed Germany's chief industrial region, millions of men had died in battle, and between 400,000 and 700,000 German civilians starved to death due to the British blockade of merchant ships, rendering the country a poor source of funds.

Regardless of these hardships, few of the nations involved in the conflict believed that World War I would actually be the "War to End All Wars," and that skepticism manifested itself in the fact that all major powers began military modernization and rearmament with the ink scarcely dry on the Versailles treaty. France proved no exception - the Third Republic instituted a program to provide France with a modern navy, among other projects.

The Washington Naval Treaty of 1922 stood in the way of this ambition, however. The victors of World War I signed this treaty with the intention of limiting the size of future navies in order to hopefully prevent any more wars. The Americans sprang the idea on their allies and other nations at the Washington, D.C. conference from which it took its name, creating absolute consternation. One British newspaper reporter present at the negotiations wrote, "It is an audacious and astonishing scheme, and took us off our feet. The few men to whom I spoke babbled incoherently. What will they say in London? To see a British First Lord of the Admiralty, and another late First Lord, sitting at a table with the American Secretary of State telling them how many ships they might keep and how many they should scrap, struck me as a delightfully fantastic idea." (Jones, 2001, 128).

Adding a touch of colorful humor to his account, the newsman also described how, when Secretary of State Hughes proposed these limits, one of the English naval officers present lunged forward abruptly "in his chair with the manner of a bulldog, sleeping on a sunny doorstep, who had been poked in the stomach by the impudent foot of an itinerant soapcanvasser [ie soap salesman]." (Jones, 2001, 128).

Hughes

Nonetheless, the Americans outlined a treaty that completely limited the total tonnage of battleships and the size of other ships, such as destroyers, without imposing a specific limit on the number that could be built. To France's great indignation, it found itself consigned to the number four position as regards naval strength, behind the UK, America, and Japan. At the same time, the British, smarting from the U-boat war, wanted to ban submarines completely, but the French, believing them a valuable resource for a second tier naval power like themselves, insisted that the low tonnage allotted to them be counterbalanced with permission to build submarines. The British eventually yielded by withdrawing their objections to submarines, which ended up not being truly covered by the Treaty (other than the fact that Germany could not build them).

The powers renewed the Treaty in 1930, but the Japanese displayed such indignation at being treated as subordinates that the Treaty had become a dead letter to them. Indeed, it was ignored by all parties by the mid-1930s.

Although the French had begun modernizing their fleet shortly after World War I ended, they strongly ramped up their efforts in 1937, when all countries fully ignored the Washington Naval Treaty. The French accompanied the buildup of their fleet with an increase in the size of their naval personnel to 160,000 men, including all ranks of service.

The French Navy viewed itself as a breed apart, which, to a considerable extent, they were. They deemed themselves apolitical, patriotic, and a model of sobriety and efficiency compared to the Army and the civilian government. This assessment, while mythologized and oversimplified, contained more than a grain of truth. They were certainly conservative, nationalistic, and displayed a considerable, though not invariable, sense of honor. According to Naval Minister Georges Leygues, who served during eight different brief, scandal-ridden civilian government administrations, "I served for fifteen or twenty years in practically every Ministry of the Republic before coming to the Navy. I found competent people everywhere. But here one is completely astounded to find his staff working indefatigably without demanding the Legion of Honor at the end of a month or a promotion at the end of three. What is most heartwarming is the Navy's discipline, loyalty, and absolutely unselfish devotion to duty!" (Auphan, 2016, 10).

Leygues

The French deployed the main portion of their battle fleet in the Mediterranean, followed by ships and subs stationed in the Atlantic Ocean. They scattered other vessels around the North Sea, and they even sent a few destroyers, submarines, and cruisers to patrol the Indochinese waters. By the time World War II began in earnest, the French fleet consisted of the following:

- 1 Aircraft Carrier
- 7 Battleships

- 12 Light Cruisers
- 7 Heavy Cruisers
- 56 Gunboats and Minesweepers
- 78 Destroyers
- 81 Submarines
- 126 support craft

Naturally, the French Navy could not mobilize this entire force immediately, but the list provides an insight into the French battle fleet's composition at the onset of the war. As with the Third Reich, the French failed to grasp the full significance of aircraft carriers, the war-winning weapons system of the new naval age. They only deployed a single aircraft carrier, the *Bearn*, which was never used in combat, much like the Kriegsmarine's *Graf Zeppelin*.

Although the French produced very well-built destroyers, their special class of ships called "counter destroyers," to be used against enemy cruisers and destroyers, lacked the heavy guns needed for their intended role, and they found themselves at a disadvantage when fighting foreign ships of equal tonnage. This was a byproduct of the fact that te main French goal in the interwar years was to remain equal in strength to the Italian navy.

The fleet saw a modicum of action – but no combat – when the Spanish Civil War broke out in 1935. As Franco's nationalists and the communist forces of the so-called "Republicans" mauled one another, France used the sea as an escape route for the many thousands of French citizens living and working in Spain, who now understandably wanted to return home rather than run the risk of being killed in the crossfire. The French Navy provided destroyer escorts for the 500 merchantmen pressed into service to effect the evacuations. However, though the then-socialist government of France plundered the armories of their own Army to send large quantities of materiel to the Soviet-backed Republicans, they understood that the conservative Navy would participate in such a scheme only grudgingly. Accordingly, the arms shipments traveled overland, seriously depleting French Army arsenals on the eve of World War II.

During the later 1930s, the French fleet received just 21% of the nation's military budget, but the navy made excellent use of it within the limitations placed by their government. Incessant maneuvers by both day and night in all weather conditions, together with constant gunnery practice, honed the skills of captains and crews. All ships received the latest radio equipment, and research into improved sonar commenced (but could not be completed prior to World War II). The fleet also stockpiled 3 million tons of fuel oil and constructed an additional 1.2 million tons' worth of massive concrete tanks.

At the eleventh hour in 1938, the Navy recognized the emerging importance of aircraft carriers. With only a single example at their disposal, the fleet ordered and paid for the construction of two more carriers that would have had a more advanced design than the *Bearn*. However, the war interrupted their building and they never saw the light of day.

The Establishment of Vichy France

When Nazi Germany invaded Poland in 1939 and conquered the nation in the first example of "Blitzkrieg," the United Kingdom and France declared war on Germany in support of their Polish ally. Though the Soviet Union also invaded Poland on September 17th, 1939, the Allies chose not to declare war on the second dictatorship, fearing its size and power.

On May 10, 1940, the Third Reich's Wehrmacht attacked France as well. Bypassing the formidable and effective Maginot Line – which, despite its later reputation, actually functioned effectively in areas where the Axis engaged it – the Germans feinted into Belgium to draw off the British and French armies stationed in northern France, then struck their main blow through the Ardennes Forest.

Heinz Guderian

The Allies believed the Ardennes impenetrable to heavy armor, but Heinz Guderian's and Erwin Rommel's panzers readily traversed the woodland and punched violently westward on a lightning campaign to the Atlantic coast. French soldiers fought bravely and sometimes effectively at specific locations, but multiple factors doomed their efforts overall. Soon, the French Army found itself collapsing and in full retreat.

The Germans themselves expressed astonishment at their degree of success, as Karl von Stackelberg, the war diarist of General Georg-Hans Reinhardt's XXXXI Panzer Corps recorded shortly after crossing the French border: "It was inexplicable. How was it possible, that after this first major battle on French territory, after this victory on the Meuse, this gigantic consequence should follow? How was it possible, these French soldiers with their officers, so completely downcast, so completely demoralized, would allow themselves to go more or less voluntarily into imprisonment?" (Horne, 2007, 271).

France suffered defeat mainly due to its slow, methodical, extremely rigid combat technique, which removed almost all initiative and flexibility from small tactical units actually engaged with the enemy. Against this parched and lumbering orthodoxy the Germans set a dynamic new method of warfare that exploited the mobility advantages of armored attack groups assisted by deadly close air support to the full. The Wehrmacht combined bold, sweeping strategic movements and deep penetration and encirclement with great tactical flexibility created by allowing junior officers maximum independence.

Staggering losses in World War I also made the French leadership reluctant to fight to the last bullet. After losing much of an entire generation of young men in the Flanders bloodbath, and suffering immense damage to their industrial heartland, French demographics and economics remained weak in 1940. Pacifism blossomed, ironically, in the right wing of French politics, as the author Roger Martin du Gard expressed in 1936: "Anything rather than war! Anything!... even Fascism in Spain... even Fascism in France: Nothing, no trial, no servitude can be compared to war: Anything, Hitler rather than war!" He was not alone - in the same year, the Provencal novelist Jean Giono wrote, "For my part, I prefer being a living German to being a dead Frenchman." (Christofferson, 2006, 11-12).

The spirit animating Vichy already existed in France during the 20 years before the regime arose. The French, appalled and hamstrung by their losses in World War I, already accepted defeat and collaboration as preferable to another bloodbath. Simultaneously, and unselfconsciously, the right wing and conservative elements blamed French lack of fighting spirit on the moral "decadence" and "decay" of modernity and urbanization. Both these themes emerged as foundational concepts of the Vichy regime, demonstrating its actuality as an organic outgrowth of interwar French culture, not an aberration from it.

This enormous rout of the French, both military and civilian, involving both the nominally powerful and the powerless, formed the milieu in which the Vichy government received its initial form: "The scale of this extraordinary population movement, christened the Exodus, astonished contemporary observers. One described it as resembling a geological cataclysm. The writer-pilot Antoine Saint-Exupéry wrote that from the air it looked as if some giant had kicked a massive anthill. It has been estimated that between 6 and 10 million people fled their homes. The population of Chartres dropped from 23,000 to 800, Lille from 200,000 to 20,000." (Jackson, 2001, 127).

The French government, soon on the retreat, found itself hard-pressed to make any decisions at all. With key individuals missing during the "Exodus" and the remaining cabinet on the move, debate and command crashed to a standstill, with occasional spasms of over-hasty attempts at leadership. Paul Reynaud, the 118th Prime Minister of France, occupied his position only two months before finding himself at the heart of this crisis. A well-meaning man who defied the Nazis and spent much of the war imprisoned at Sachsenhausen Concentration Camp and Itter Castle, Reynaud made several critical appointments with a strong bearing on the immediate future of France, for both good and ill.

Paul Reynaud

Attempting to patch up disintegrating French morale, Reynaud ousted officials perceived as weak and placed more energetic men in their place. Charles de Gaulle, then an aggressive and fearless tank commander who had long advocated modern, Blitzkrieg-style tactics, received a promotion to Brigadier General and an appointment as Undersecretary of War, making him prominent enough to launch his coming political career as leader of the Free French during World War II and France itself postwar.

Charles de Gaulle

Reynaud also appointed the fiercely right-wing Major General Maxime Weygand to the post of Supreme Commander of the French Army, too late to accomplish anything besides further confusion in the deliquescing command structure. He also named Marshal Philippe Petain as the Minister of State on May 18th, 1940, hoping to bolster morale through the old general's undeniable bravery, fame, and charisma. Both Petain and Weygand became linchpins of the emergent Vichy state.

Philippe Petain

On May 25, a French official proposed an armistice with the Germans, just 15 days after the first panzer rumbled across the frontier. Weygand, meanwhile, managed to stiffen resistance briefly and delay the Germans for several days with a defense in depth along several major axes of advance. Nevertheless, the French government abandoned Paris on June 10, proclaiming it an "open city" to spare its potential devastation.

Maxime Weygand

The British Expeditionary Force's evacuation from Dunkirk in late May and early June enabled them to fight on, but it enraged both Weygand and Petain against the United Kingdom, inclining both towards making an accommodation with Germany. The government moved to Tours, and there, on June 12, General Weygand again proposed an armistice with the Germans. Other suggestions included shifting the remains of the French Army and government to the colonial holdings in North Africa, maintaining independence there and using that as a springboard for an eventual return if the British (and possibly the Americans) ever managed a continental offensive.

At this point, with France on the verge of total collapse, Churchill attempted to shore up the continental nation with a remarkable suggestion too often forgotten in history books. He suggested a Franco-British Union on June 16, 1940, which would unite the two countries into one. The French and British Parliaments would merge, all citizens would enjoy one common citizenship, and the French and English army leadership would form a War Cabinet having equal control over a unified military. Sir Orme Sargent put the case for this astonishing proposition forcefully: "[S]uch a system of close and permanent cooperation between France and Great Britain – political, military, and economic – as will for all practical purposes make of the two countries a single unit […] Such a unit would constitute an effective counterweight to 80 million Germans in the middle of Europe." (Shlaim, 1974, 31).

Churchill's suggestion, though well-received by many of the French, failed to carry the day in part because Reynaud, embarrassed by the confusion of his cabinet, neglected to invite the charismatic man to the meeting where his government discussed that very matter. Without Churchill's forceful personality, and with many of the French officials believing his absence "treachery" (rather than ignorance of the meeting thanks to Reynaud's error), support for the

Franco-British Union waned.

Churchill

When the Germans took Paris on June 14, Reynaud's government retreated from Tours to Bordeaux. Reynaud attempted to gain an assurance of assistance from President Franklin D. Roosevelt, though the eventual response naturally proved negative in the face of the American public's pacifism. In the meantime, Weygand refused any course except armistice, wanting to preserve French military honor.

At this critical juncture, Deputy Premier Camille Chautemps made the fateful suggestion that the French government find out what terms the Germans offered for an armistice, without actually negotiating with them. This gave the "armistice faction" of Petain and Weygand 13 members out of the 19 forming Reynaud's cabinet.

Deeply saddened and despairing, Reynaud resigned as Prime Minister late on the 16th. This automatically led to Petain, as Minister of State, rising to become head of the French government.

The other French leaders underestimated Petain, believing him senile at age 83. Instead, the Marshal showed remarkable vigor, acumen, and slyness, along with a robust physique for a man of his age. Though he played a quiet role in the days before his ascension to the head of the French government, this largely represented a pose over a canny and keenly ambitious mind seizing the chance to pounce on the reins of power.

Events in France continued unfolding rapidly. On June 17, Petain announced the armistice before its actual signing, leading many to believe it a *fait accompli*. On the 18th, Hitler informed Mussolini that he would receive very little French territory – essentially only a few small towns near the border his men seized during the fighting. For the most part, Mussolini's untrained and ill-equipped soldiers bloodied themselves valiantly but uselessly against the Alpine Maginot Line, while their Duce heaped scorn on them for a situation objectively due entirely to his poor decisions.

Petain Meeting Hitler

General Charles Leon Huntziger, later commander in chief of Vichy ground forces and who died in an airplane accident in 1941, met with Hitler himself on June 22, 1940 to negotiate the actual terms of the armistice. The negotiations, of course, consisted of the Germans dictating terms and the French accepting them. To further underline their dominance, the Germans chose the Compiegne Wagon as the scene for the ceremony. This railway car, used as an office by French Marshal Ferdinand Foch in World War I, served as the venue for Germany's signing of the armistice ending the first global conflict in 1918. Huntziger now signed the armistice acknowledging French defeat in the same carriage, at the town of Rethondes. The Waffen SS demolished the Compiegne Wagon, then a trophy in Crawinkel, Germany, in March 1945 using explosives, thus preventing its recapture by the Allies.

Hitler soon left the negotiations in the hands of Generaloberst Wilhelm Keitel. The terms of the 24-article armistice proved comprehensive. The Germans designated an Occupation Zone encompassing approximate 60% of France's land area, including the country's industrial north, Paris, and the entire Atlantic seaboard down to the Spanish border. The Unoccupied Zone – soon to be the French State or "Vichy France" – included the remaining 40% of the nation in the southeast, except for a few slivers of territory granted to Mussolini.

Wilhelm Keitel

Other terms included the creation of a small, impotent "Army of the Armistice," the automatic remanding of political refugees in Vichy territory to German custody, and the holding of 1.5 million French POWs in Germany as slave labor and hostages. The Third Reich threw the French a few crumbs, such as the retention of their fleet in their own Mediterranean ports and continued ownership of their overseas colonies. The Germans insisted that the French disarm their fleet and disband most of its personnel, however.

Huntziger initially rejected these terms and engineers from both sides rigged a telephone line permitting a direct conversation between Keitel and Weygand. Weygand also attempted to soften the terms, but met with a stony rebuff from Keitel. The Germans held all the trump cards and the French must acquiesce or suffer total subjugation.

Weygand only agreed to leave 1.5 million POWs in German hands because he believed that England would fall within 3 weeks, ending the war and freeing the prisoners. The Armistice also made Vichy France liable for the (then unspecified) costs of paying for the German occupation forces in the Occupied Zone. The Germans left to the French the option to determine the exact form of government, location of the French State's capital, and other details of government and social organization in the "Free Zone." Faced with an ultimatum, Weygand authorized Huntziger to sign at 6:50 PM on June 23rd.

The American journalist William Shirer, present in the Wagon during the negotiations, took down a personal statement by Huntziger after the signing. The defeated French general, his voice quaking with emotion, said, "I declare that the French Government has ordered me to sign these terms of armistice… Forced by the fate of arms to cease the struggle in which we were engaged on the side of the Allies, France sees imposed on her very hard conditions. France has the right to expect in the future negotiations that Germany show a spirit which will permit the two great neighboring countries to live and work in peace." (Shirer, 2011, 728).

While all of this was taking place, a minor French cabinet minister, Brigadier General Charles de Gaulle, recently appointed Under-Secretary of State for National Defense and War, was engaged in liaison with the British in the formation of a joint Anglo-French war strategy. As Pétain entered into armistice negotiations with the Germans, de Gaulle, who had for months been urging a revision of French military strategy and the modernization of the French Army, decided not to participate, instead returning to London. With neither specific agenda nor official sanction, de Gaulle determined that he, on behalf of the French nation, would not acknowledge surrender. The Battle of France had been lost, that much was inescapable, but French sovereignty need not be surrendered.

In Churchill, de Gaulle found a sympathetic ear. What, precisely, would emerge from supporting this aloof and rather austere French general, Churchill could not guess, but his instincts told him that de Gaulle, for all his lack of charm, spoke for the fading embers of a greater France. Permission was granted to de Gaulle to address the French nation on June 18, 1940, using the facilities of the British Broadcasting Corporation. That evening, his voice, little known in France at the time, was heard, urging a rejection of the armistice and a continuation of the resistance.

This speech, known as the June 18 Appeal, was not widely heard on the day of its delivery, since the nation of France was preoccupied at the time with the shock of defeat and machinations of the new French government to reach accommodations with the Nazis. However, it was lodged in the archive of French consciousness, and, for the first time, the name de Gaulle entered the political lexicon of a demoralized nation. His name would begin to grow in stature as the seeds of resistance took root.

Initially, beyond this rather theoretical legitimacy of British recognition (even the United States had recognized Vichy), the exiled French in Britain kept de Gaulle and his apparent pretensions at arm's length. No doubt, his unattractive personality contributed something to this; the authoritarian impression in his personal embodiment of French independence irritated many, which ensured the Free French Committee did not rise to anywhere near the expectations initially placed upon it. Likewise, de Gaulle's efforts to form a Free French Army fell short of expectations. Of the few thousand French soldiers in London, many had evacuated from Dunkirk alongside British troops, but only 10% of them signed up to fight for Free France. Others chose to join British forces directly, while the majority opted for repatriation back to France. According to contemporary British estimates, Free French forces comprised 4,000 soldiers, 1,000 sailors, and some 150 airmen at the most.

On June 19, 1940, the day after the June 18 Appeal, de Gaulle broadcast a second message to the people of France, stating that all forms of legitimate authority in France had disappeared and all institutions had ceased to function. It was, he went on to urge, the clear duty of all French servicemen to fight on. The legal merits of this statement have been the subject of debate ever since. The question was whether de Gaulle had represented the legal continuation of the French government, or whether he stood at the helm of a revolutionary movement. Neither Vichy France nor de Gaulle referred to the Republic—now suspended—directly, which posed a third option as to whether both had been illegitimate.

In response to this dilemma, at least among those French citizens who had been aware of it, most, including the majority of French troops in Britain, opted to align themselves with Vichy. Initially, de Gaulle attracted very few French servicemen to Free France, mostly due to the belief that Britain could not survive the Nazi onslaught in the summer of 1940. The commander of armed forces under Vichy, General Maxime Weygand, was heard to remark soon after the signing of the armistice that "England will have her neck wrung like a chicken within two weeks." After emerging victorious in the Battle of Britain, Churchill would famously refer to that prediction in a speech before the Canadian Parliament: "On top of all this came the great French catastrophe. The French Army collapsed, and the French nation was dashed into utter and, as it has so far proved, irretrievable confusion. The French Government had at their own suggestion solemnly bound themselves with us not to make a separate peace. It was their duty and it was also their interest to go to North Africa, where they would have been at the head of the French Empire. In Africa, with our aid, they would have had overwhelming sea power. They would have had the recognition of the United States, and the use of all the gold they had lodged beyond the seas. If they had done this Italy might have been driven out of the war before the end of 1940, and France would have held her place as a nation in the counsels of the Allies and at the conference table of the victors. But their generals misled them. When I warned them that Britain would fight on alone whatever they did, their generals told their Prime Minister and his divided Cabinet, 'In three weeks England will have her neck wrung like a chicken.' Some chicken! Some neck!"

On June 24, 1940, de Gaulle turned his attention to France's colonies, urging French servicemen posted overseas to join him. The only ranking French officer to respond to the call was Vice-Admiral Émile Muselier, who made his appearance in London a week later, flying in on a British aircraft from Gibraltar. On July 1, de Gaulle named Muselier commander of Free French Naval Forces, the Navales Françaises Libres, and provisional commander of the Free

French Air Force, Forces Aériennes Françaises Libres. On the same day, Muselier issued his own appeal to French sailors and pilots stationed abroad to join the embryonic service, establishing a general staff, initially comprised of only French Ship-of-the-Line-Captain Georges Thierry d'Argenlieu and the ship Voisin.

Georges Thierry d'Argenlieu was a curious character. A Carmelite friar as well as a naval captain, it was he who had suggested the adoption of the Cross of Lorraine as the symbol of Free France. This was in reference to the devotion and commitment of Joan of Arc, the patron saint of France, whose symbol it had been, and the fact it served as a strong alternative symbol to the Nazi swastika, while maintaining the same bold expression and nationalistic allusion.

Georges Thierry d'Argenlieu

At the time France surrendered, the French fleet was widely dispersed, with ships berthed in the French naval port of Toulon, Mers El Kébir in Algeria, and in various ports scattered across the French empire overseas. Some had escaped from French control, seeking refuge in British ports and in the Egyptian port of Alexandria. At the launch of Operation Catapult, the Royal Naval operation against Mers El Kébir, the ships sanctuaried in British ports were boarded and commandeered by British personnel, including the French submarine *Surcouf*, which had arrived in Portsmouth immediately following the occupation. At the same time, the reluctance of French naval crews to put their ships under the authority of Vichy France did not necessarily imply a willingness or interest in handing them over to either British or Free French command. There was resistance over the takeover of the *Surcouf*, resulting in the death of two British officers and a French sailor.[1] The ships escaping the action at Mers El Kébir took refuge at the French naval base in Toulon, where the bulk of the French fleet resided under Vichy command, but they were uninvolved in Allied or Axis naval operations.

In the weeks before the German occupation, the French aircraft carrier *Béarn*, along with the light cruisers *Jeanne d'Arc* and *Émile Bertin*, detached from the main fleet and sailed to Canada with the Bank of France's gold bullion onboard, intended for safekeeping. From Canada, the *Béarn* sailed to the United States, where it took a consignment of new military aircraft ordered by the French before the occupation onboard. En route back across the Atlantic, the armistice was signed, so the ship was diverted to the French Caribbean island of Martinique, where it joined several other French ships interned at the insistence of the United States.

The aviation arm of the Free French Navy, the Aéronavale française libre, was formed at more or less the same time. It operated all French naval aircraft, seaplanes, and flying boats escaping from German-occupied France, with the addition of naval aircraft from the French colonies declaring allegiance to de Gaulle, as well as aircraft donated to the service by the British and Americans.

The Free French Air Force, Forces Aériennes Françaises Libres, was founded on the basis of 10 French airmen who took off from the Bordeaux-Mérignac Airfield on June 17, 1940, five days before the signing of the armistice. They arrived in Britain declaring allegiance to de Gaulle and Free France. To this was added a small contingent of expatriate Frenchmen and adventurers from Chile, Argentina, and Uruguay, all seeking active duty in the war. From a strength of only 500 on the eve of the Free France formation to some 900—including 200 aviators—by 1941, the Forces Aériennes Françaises Libres was initially the most robustly supported branch of the Free French Armed Forces. In the summer of 1940, General de Gaulle named then Colonel Martial Henri Valin as commander-in-chief of the Forces Aériennes Françaises Libres.

The Vichy Fleet

While the British would blame the French for their lack of fight in 1940, it should be recalled that France had not yet recovered from the demographic disaster of World War I. France lost a higher proportion of its young men than nearly any other power in the war, leading to a greatly decreased birthrate, a population slump, and a corresponding contraction of the economy.

All of this lasted for many years, and neither the French government nor the French military had the stomach for another extermination of their young men, especially for the sake of Poland, which was unlikely to be helped by that sacrifice in any case. French resistance collapsed rapidly not through lack of courage, but through absence of motivation. Provided the Germans offered acceptable terms, it seemed more prudent to end the conflict quickly rather than spend months or years wiping out their own population through wartime attrition, with the same result probable at

---

[1] The deaths took place during a brief shootout and bayonet fight in wardroom of the *Surcouf* as the British boarding party confronted the French crew while the submarine was moored in Devonport, England.

the end in any case.

Most importantly for the French Navy, the Armistice terms included the following statement: "The German government solemnly declares that during the war it does not intend to use for its own purposes the French War Fleet stationed in ports under German control, apart from units needed for coast-guarding and minesweeping. It further declares [...] that it does not intend to

The Germans demanded that the French fleet remain in its ports until the conclusion of the conflict, which Hitler believed would come before September 1940. Petain believed that the English would soon succumb to the Wehrmacht and stated his position succinctly: "To make union with England is fusion with a corpse."

When the war had started, the majority of the French fleet lay at anchor at ports in the Mediterranean Sea, but a portion of the fleet made its way to the Atlantic to assist the British. In the late 1930s, the British and French fleets often worked in close cooperation, establishing channels of communication and a good deal of mutual understanding between the officers of the two services, despite the fact these good relations did not extend to their respective governments and high naval commands, whose rarefied positions put them out of touch with the world of ordinary fighting captains and admirals. This mutual respect and understanding would only add to the tragedy of Operation Catapult, when the men actually involved on both sides understood the total senselessness of the situation but found themselves compelled to act in accordance with their orders anyway.

The head of the fleet, Francois Darlan, had little liking for the British but proved a fairly able leader considering the limitations of his situation. During the Armistice negotiations and at every point thereafter, he provided the English with whatever information he could and his repeated assurances that he would send the fleet to harbors in Africa, out of reach of the Germans. He and other top French naval officers repeatedly asserted that they would destroy their vessels rather than let them fall into Third Reich hands; the eventual outcome proved they spoke the truth.

Darlan

Darlan's actions also indicated that he had no intention of handing the fleet over to German control, as the ships under construction and capable of sailing, such as the *Richelieu,* departed French ports for Africa immediately. Those not yet able to sail were scuttled rather than giving the Germans the ability to appropriate them. French naval personnel thoroughly destroyed them with explosives, then demolished most of the port facilities at Cherbourg and Brest, which would be in the German occupation zone.

These actions and assurances did not satisfy Churchill, however. He quickly developed an almost fanatical dedication to seeing the French fleet forced to either scuttle itself immediately or be destroyed outright by a British naval attack, an attack which would, under current circumstances, be carried out against a neutral nation. Unless the Vichy state decided to bend over backwards (which, in fact, it did, though little to its ultimate benefit), an attack would represent an act of war that might push the French firmly into the Axis camp.

In the wake of the French surrender, three important British admirals – Sir James Fownes Somerville (eventually tasked with destroying part of the French fleet), Sir Andrew Cunningham, and Sir Dudley Pound – all argued against Churchill's plan and repeatedly urged him to abandon his purpose. All had dealt closely with the French during the interwar years and knew from experience that Darlan meant what he said when assuring the British he would not allow the fleet to be captured by the Germans.

Somerville

Cunningham

Pound

Nevertheless, Churchill remained adamant. Perhaps he was hoping to impress the Americans with his firmness, or maybe he was angry that the French had adopted neutrality rather than allowing their country to be immolated after the British Expeditionary Force left it. He insisted that the French either hand their ships over to the British (which would have incurred the wrath of the Germans), sink them, or see them sunk by hostile British action.

Darlan refused to hand his ships over to the English without orders from Petain, much the same way he refused to hand them over to the Germans. For his part, Petain would not issue such orders since his primary goal was to prevent the devastation of France, not give the British a gift of warships at the expense of his own countrymen's blood.

In response, Churchill ordered that Somerville take a group of warships – Task Force H – to the North African port of Mers-el-Kebir, where multiple French battleships, battlecruisers, and destroyers now lay at anchor, and force their destruction in one way or another.

The Start of Operation Catapult

Admiral Marcel-Bruno Gensoul, in command of the French vessels anchored at Mers-el-Kebir, remained alert even after the signing of the Armistice ceded control of northern France to Germany and organized the rest of the country into the neutral Vichy French nation. The harbor actually represented a poor choice for modern warships, due to the shape of the bottom and its general configuration. Thus, the only choice for long-term anchorage was to position the large ships on the inner side of the jetty blocking much of the harbor mouth, with their prows pointing towards land. This placed them at a huge and awkward disadvantage because their powerful forward batteries could not fire on any ships approaching from the sea, and only the rearmost turret faced the direction of primary danger.

Perhaps even worse, the ships' positions partially trapped them in the harbor. The correct position would have been mooring on the outer side of the jetty, where they could not only fire easily on approaching threats but simply accelerate out to sea directly for combat maneuvers or escape. As it stood, they would need to make a turn and maneuver around the jetty – through a chokepoint – in order to reach the open ocean, placing them under the guns of an attacker for an extended period.

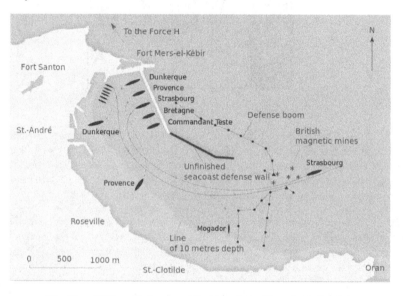

Max Ross O'Manchin's map of the French positions in the harbor

Initially, Gensoul anticipated the possibility of an Italian attack as the most likely threat. He did not entirely trust the Italians – the main maritime rivals of the French – to respect an Armistice devised and signed by the Germans and then presented as a *fait accompli* to their Italian allies. His alarm rose higher when a delegation of swaggering Italians arrived, brimming over with predatory jocularity at the defeat of France, and compelled him to sign a copy of the Armistice on June 24, 1940, two days after the original signing.

The Italians, however, would respect the terms of the Armistice for the time being. They left with their documents, but just a few hours later, the long, lean, pale gray shape of a British destroyer appeared in the sea off Mers-el-Kebir. This proved even more jarring to Gensoul, and with good reason. The British had not signaled ahead but instead merely appeared, specter-like, from the ocean.

The intruder proved to be the HMS *Douglas,* a *Scott*-class destroyer dating to the end of World War I. The ship carried Admiral Sir Dudley North, Flag Officer North Atlantic (FOCNA) at Gibraltar. With France now officially a neutral country, Gensoul could not allow a warship of a combatant power to linger in a French naval harbor. However, he allowed Admiral North to come aboard to say whatever he wished to, giving him 20 minutes to come to the point.

The HMS *Douglas*

North duly arrived on the *Dunkerque* and met with Gensoul. Speaking in a friendly manner, the Englishman came to the point immediately, repeating the usual mantra urging the French naval vessels to sail to Britain, where they would be safe from the Germans. Gensoul, as a correct and loyal military man, replied that he would remain in Mers-el-Kebir until he received contrary orders from his government, and that in the meantime North could reassure himself that the French had already emplaced scuttling charges and would sink their ships if the Axis attempted to commandeer them. North seemingly accepted this, took a cordial farewell of his Gallic counterpart, and boarded the *Douglas* to sail back to Gibraltar.

The *Dunkerque*

The danger seemed to have passed from the French perspective, but in fact, nothing could be further from the case. By this time, Admiral Somerville had arrived in Gibraltar, under orders that came directly from Churchill himself to deal with the Vichy ships if capitulation did not prove forthcoming. Force H had also come, specifically to take over Mediterranean patrol duties in the absence of the French, but now likely to be used for a more ominous purpose also.

While the French went about their daily routines in the harbor of Mers-el-Kebir, the British prepared to carry out Churchill's orders to capture or destroy the vessels. All three English admirals involved remained reluctant at the prospect of attacking the very men who had been their allies through years of naval cooperation, and who almost certainly represented no threat to the British. Nonetheless, they stood prepared to do their duty.

On June 29, a British seaplane left Gibraltar and flew to Mers-el-Kebir. The French spotted it almost immediately in the blue Algerian sky and watched it uneasily. The British aircraft flew low over the harbor, circling slowly and repeatedly. These were obvious signs of a photoreconnaissance mission. The French officers observing, including Gensoul, knew that the British were taking photographs of the ships and defenses, and that such reconnaissance frequently formed the prelude to an attack.

The French were further unnerved when the plane returned the next day, June 30. Once again, it swept over the harbor and port defenses in slow arcs, clearly collecting more intelligence. The French held their fire, and in observance of the terms of the Armistice, they did not send their available aircraft aloft to chase the nosy Britons away.

Though the French did not know it since they lacked operational sonar, two British submarines cruised on patrol off the mouth of the Mers-el-Kebir harbor as well. These surfaced out of sight of the French installations or at night when necessary, and otherwise remained at periscope depth to watch for attempts by the French ships to flee. These two submarines, the *Pandora* and *Proteus*, carried the relatively advanced Mark VIII 21-inch torpedo thanks being part of the

Parthian-class.

Another brief lull followed, but Gensoul's fleet now had only a matter of hours of peace left to them. Force H under Somerville left Gibraltar late at night, under cover of darkness, lessening the chance that spies would observe it and warn the Vichy force. The photographs brought back by the seaplane gave the British admiral and his captains precise knowledge of the French ships' locations and their vulnerability.

Somerville and North talked in Gibraltar prior to the former's departure. The discussion took place in Somerville's day cabin on the HMS *Hood,* under twin portraits of King George VI and Queen Elizabeth. Captain Cedric "Hooky" Holland of the *Ark Royal* aircraft carrier, slated to serve as the interpreter and chief negotiator thanks to his fluency in French, also attended the small meeting, as did several other officers, including Vice Admiral Commanding Aircraft Carriers Sir Lionel "Nutty" Wells. North stressed that Somerville should absolutely not use force against the French, since doing so could easily transform Vichy France from a neutral country into an active, willing member of the Axis in the name of achieving revenge. North quipped that Operation Catapult might better bear the name of Operation Boomerang because it could easily fly back and hit them instead.

The HMS *Hood*

With the backing of his fellow naval officers, and feeling that he would be dishonoring his service by carrying out such an attack, Somerville actually wired the Admiralty on the afternoon before his departure to urge them to reconsider. The Admiralty's top brass mulled the recommendation, but ultimately they lacked the nerve to confront Churchill and his War Cabinet on the matter. Accordingly, they signaled back that Somerville should carry out the mission as already planned.

Somerville now understood that his orders obliged him to use violence if French capitulation did not occur quickly after the British arrived. Dreading the necessity of firing on men he effectively viewed as comrades to carry out an order he deemed ill-advised and completely unnecessary, Somerville left Gibraltar with Force H in a bleak mood. Churchill sent a message to him directly shortly before his departure via telegraph: "You are charged with one of the most difficult and disagreeable tasks that a British admiral has ever been faced with. But we have complete confidence in you and rely on you to carry it out relentlessly." (Smith, 2009, 54).

Fruitless Negotiations

Somerville sailed on Force H's flagship, the HMS *Hood,* a battlecruiser destined to be annihilated by a catastrophic magazine explosion in May 1941 while in combat with the colossal Kriegsmarine battleship *Bismarck.* Two other battleships, the *Resolution* and the *Valiant,* accompanied the *Hood.* A single aircraft carrier, *Ark Royal,* provided air support. Two light cruisers, *Arethusa* and *Enterprise,* and 11 destroyers – *Active, Escort, Faulknor, Foxhound, Fearless, Forester, Foresight, Keppel, Vidette, Vortigern,* and *Wrestler* – rounded out the task force's roster.

Task Force H arrived off Mers-el-Kebir (known to the British simply as Oran) early on the morning of July 3, 1940. While the larger ships hung back discreetly, the destroyer HMS *Foxhound* glided up to the steel torpedo net strung at the entrance to the harbor. There the destroyer came to a stop, hidden from the French by a morning mist that lay over the ocean's placid surface, and there it lurked unseen for the next several hours.

The *Foxhound*

The French ships stirred to life and men lined up for their morning coffee and pastries. Gensoul's officers, faced with thousands of idle young men chafing at their confinement in port, had planned a rather festive array of activities for the day. This included games of water polo, followed by boat races, then swimming races to finish the day's entertainment. For any men not exhausted by this highly physical selection of sports, shore leave to visit Oran's taverns and brothels remained as likely evening entertainment.

The French continued their daily routine until 9:30 a.m., when the brilliant sun finally cleared the ocean mist enough to reveal the *Foxhound* riding on the gentle swell just outside the harbor. An ensign, Jean-Paul Bezard, first spotted the Royal Navy warship from his station on the *Mogador*-class destroyer *Volta*. Bezard raised the alarm, the officers ordered general quarters sounded the bugles, and men hurried to recall the large numbers of sailors then enjoying the day's first boat race to their stations.

With the sudden activity around the French ships making clear that they had been spotted, the British on board the anchored destroyer began using their Morse code signal lamp to communicate with the French beyond the jetty. The *Ark Royal*'s captain, Cedric Holland, was on the *Foxhound* and, with his knowledge of French, provided the text which the signal lamp operators flashed over to their counterparts in Gensoul's fleet.

The British first identified their vessel and requested permission to enter the harbor for negotiations, standard procedure for such cases. However, Holland then appended a longer and more menacing message. This message, sent by signal lamp, reached every French ship's signaler. These men quickly passed the gist of the communication to the crew on their ship, and it was clear the British intended to frighten and demoralize the French sailors as much as possible: "THE BRITISH ADMIRALTY HAS SENT CAPTAIN HOLLAND TO CONFER WITH YOU – STOP – THE BRITISH NAVY HOPES THAT THEIR PROPOSALS WILL ENABLE YOU AND THE VALIANT AND GLORIOUS FRENCH NAVY TO BE BY OUR SIDE – STOP – IN THESE CIRCUMSTANCES YOUR SHIPS SHOULD REMAIN YOURS AND NO ONE NEED HAVE ANXIETY FOR THE FUTURE – STOP – A BRITISH FLEET IS AT SEA OFF ORAN WAITING TO WELCOME YOU – STOP." (Smith, 2009, 56).

After a delay, Gensoul sent back a message that the *Foxhound* could enter the harbor. Holland balked at this, however, because once inside the harbor itself the destroyer could not easily flee if the French decided to seize it. Accordingly, Holland and several selected officers and men climbed down into a motor launch and puttered into the harbor in rather unspectacular fashion. Gensoul, not the most imaginative man, nevertheless managed a rather witty barb when he learned that Captain Holland had arrived to speak with him rather than Admiral North: "The first time they sent me a Vice Admiral. Today it is a Captain; tomorrow it will be a midshipman." (Smith, 2009, 57).

Somewhat miffed at this apparent demotion of his value, Gensoul decided to send Lieutenant Bernard Dufay, a tall, thin, intelligent man, to talk with Holland. However, to increase his dignity, Gensoul lent Dufay his magnificently decorated and gilded admiral's barge to sail to meet the Englishman. Dufay also spoke good English and was an acquaintance and friend of Holland's from the days of the two navies' cooperation.

This cumbersome arrangement ensured that the negotiations took even longer than would otherwise be the case. Every time some new point arose, Dufay motored the barge back to Gensoul's flagship, received fresh instructions, and then motored back to Holland's launch. Holland, knowing that he had an absolute deadline of 3:00 p.m. to persuade the French to yield in one way or another, grew more nervous and impatient as time went on.

While the parlay continued, "Nutty" Wells and his officers dispatched squadrons of Skua and Swordfish aircraft from the *Ark Royal*'s flight deck to sweep the ocean in various directions. The men aboard these planes kept a keen eye out for both submarines – clearly visible from the air in good weather if running close below the surface – and other naval forces, such as elements of the fairly dangerous Italian navy.

During the first exchange, Holland's and Dufay's crews tied their boats to a buoy so that they would not drift off in the current. Holland asked to see Gensoul personally but Dufay refused outright, telling the Englishman he would use force to prevent the motor launch's closer approach to the flagship unless Gensoul issued a different order later. Holland, on edge about the possible repercussions of the negotiations should they fail, forgot his considerable French language skills in the stress of the moment, and the two men had to confer purely in English. The heat grew intense, with the fierce glare of the North African sun beating up off the water surface as well as down from the cloudless sky. Each time Dufay approached, Holland transferred temporarily over to the barge, whose interior proved somewhat cooler than the fully exposed English motorboat.

Unable to persuade Dufay to let him approach the *Dunkerque,* Holland gave the French lieutenant a long, sealed letter to take to his chief. Much of this message consisted of a long-winded justification of Britain's political position leading to Operation Catapult, and it effectively had no use except to waste time in translation. Gensoul, an admiral in time of war, had no interest in exploring the political explanations of foreigners posing a threat with a naval force larger than his own.

The meat of the communication consisted of the following passage:

"His Majesty's Government have instructed me to demand that the French Fleet now at Mers el Kebir and Oran shall act in accordance with one of the following alternatives;

(a) Sail with us and continue the fight until victory against the Germans.

(b) Sail with reduced crews under our control to a British port. The reduced crews would be repatriated at the earliest moment. If either of these courses is adopted by you we will restore your ships to France at the conclusion of the war or pay full compensation if they are damaged meanwhile.

(c) Alternatively, if you feel bound to stipulate that your ships should not be used against the Germans lest they break the Armistice, then sail them with us with reduced crews to some French port in the West Indies —Martinique for instance— where they can be demilitarised to our satisfaction, or perhaps be entrusted to the United States and remain safe until the end of the war, the crews being repatriated. If you refuse these fair offers, I must with profound regret, require you to sink your ships within 6 hours. Finally, failing the above, I have orders from His Majesty's Government to use whatever force may be necessary to prevent your ships from falling into German or Italian hands (Lacouture, 1991, 247).

Gensoul, busy issuing orders to his captains to prepare for a likely attack, waded as quickly as possible through the political tract and skimmed the actual demands. He then ordered a message sent as quickly as possible by radio to French admiralty headquarters, where, he hoped, Admiral Darlan could read the message immediately and respond: "English force comprising three battleships, an aircraft carrier, cruisers and destroyers off Oran. Ultimatum sent: Sink your ships in six hours or we shall use force. Reply: French ships will reply to force with force." (Tute, 2007, 89).

Arguably, Gensoul potentially contributed to the impending disaster by providing only the worst alternative offered by the British message. On the other hand, given the invariable position of Darlan and the rest of the Vichy Navy to previous approaches, it remains extremely doubtful that Darlan would have authorized the scuttling, British impounding, or American impounding of the warships anyway. Made under threat of force to an as-yet undefeated naval force, all such demands – contrary to the orders of the Vichy government, to which Gensoul and Darlan still remained loyal – would likely have been met by an obdurate refusal in any case.

As it turned out, Darlan proved to be unreachable for an extended length of time. The approach of the British to Mers-el-Kebir came at the worst possible moment from the viewpoint of the Vichy naval command. Naval headquarters was at that precise moment engaged in moving from one location to another one better suited to the Navy's current role, and communications, which were already quite shaky, suffered even greater delays due to this. In fact, it took the alarmed naval staff onshore over two hours to find Darlan and send his reply to Gensoul.

In the meantime, Gensoul attempted to buy some time by writing out a message for Dufay to take back to Holland. Using a pencil, he dashed off the following message in French on a pink-papered signal pad:

> 1st. The assurances given by Admiral Gensoul to Admiral Sir Dudley North are still intact. In no case should the French vessels fall intact into the hands of Germans ("aux mains des Allemands") or Italians.
>
> 2nd. Given the substance and form of the veritable ultimatum handed to Admiral Gensoul, the French ships will defend themselves by force." (Lormier, 2007, 44).

Dufay made yet another trip back to the buoy, but only after giving orders to one of the gun turrets on the *Dunkerque* to fire on and sink Holland's motorboat if it attempted to reach the French flagship. By now, the time was 12:30 p.m., and only two and a half hours remained before the British ultimatum would expire.

In the meantime, Churchill, in a great ferment to hear of the sinking of Gensoul's ships, peppered Somerville with increasingly querulous messages asking why nothing had yet been accomplished. Somerville felt the pressure and critical undertone of Churchill's barrage of communiques, but, having nothing material to report, he did not reply. This, in turn, only made Churchill more impatient.

Back on the barge together, Holland and Dufay continued verbally fencing. Holland suddenly played something of an ace in the hole by revealing that the British knew of the three secret French naval codes that would trigger the "fighting to the last" order against any enemy designated by the government, with the intention of never surrendering a ship intact. Dufay did not bother to deny the existence of these orders, and the men reached another impasse.

By this point, under the strain of the situation, sweat starting pouring off Holland's face. Dufay observed his pallor and shaking, and he felt a certain embarrassment at witnessing the other man's condition. A brief pause followed. Then Holland tried a new tack, stating that he believed the French when they said they would not hand over their ships willingly to the Germans. But, he pointed out, how would they prevent the Germans from taking them if they remained within reach? Vichy France could not hope to withstand the full power of the Wehrmacht if the Germans came for them. Dufay responded that the French had planned for such a contingency and the Germans would not capture their ships intact.

Both men knew that the diplomatic fencing represented an exercise in futility, but their duty demanded that they carry it on to the full extent possible in any case. Holland now gave Dufay some typed notes to take to Gensoul, and he further urged Dufay to convey Britain's concerns about the Germans seizing the ships.

Dutifully, Dufay turned his barge around and once again motored across the harbor to the massive *Dunkerque*, where men on deck busied themselves with preparing the powerful ship for combat or flight. Several aircraft from *Ark Royal* now orbited steadily overhead, keeping a close eye on the actions of the French. All of the warship crews now clearly worked feverishly at the same task of preparation as the men on the *Dunkerque*.

Dufay climbed back aboard the flagship and brought the typewritten notes to Gensoul. Gensoul began reading, but he stopped when Dufay told him about the British fear that the Germans would take the ships. The admiral muttered something about the British thinking the French too incompetent to scuttle their own ships, and added a rhetorical query as to whether Holland had made the comment as a deliberate insult to the French.

By this point, Dufay's temper had started to fray under the repetitive strain and frustration, to the extent that he dared to suggest to the admiral that he either refuse the British terms or send someone else of higher rank to deal with Holland. Gensoul, likely growing weary of the endless farce himself, dashed off another handwritten note to Holland and gave it to Dufay. The French lieutenant made one final trip to the buoy and handed over the scrap of paper to his British friend. Gensoul's note calmly stated that his position had not changed, and that the French would defend themselves if necessary. He ended with a polite reminder of the possible consequences, telling the British that "the first shot fired against us will have the result of immediately putting the whole French fleet against Great Britain, a result which is diametrically opposite to that which H.M. government is seeking." (Smith, 2009, 59).

Holland said that he would need to confer with Somerville, and the two men took their leave of one another. Holland's motorboat finally coughed to life again and droned away across the hot blue water towards the *Foxhound*. Dufay returned to his own ship to await further orders from the admiral.

Astonishingly, Gensoul placed so much faith in the friendship of the British and their unwillingness to fire on the French that he ordered his men to leave action stations, though the ships' boilers continued to run. His remarks to his staff seemed to indicate he thought it would be possible to keep the British busy with negotiations until nightfall, then steam out of the port under cover of darkness, thus avoiding confrontation.

The mood of the average sailor on the French ships proved less sanguine. The signalers on each French ship had been watching and copying down the signal lamp messages passing between *Foxhound* and the British capital ships. They quickly realized the British were threatening to attack and did not hesitate to tell the ordinary crewmen near them of this fact. Within an hour or two, the news had spread to almost the entire crew, enraging most of the French seamen. The anger of the sailors grew so intense that they manned many of the anti-aircraft guns and prepared them to fire, intending to shoot down the circling British aircraft. Only with great difficulty did the French officers manage to restrain their men from taking this step. Unable to shoot down the English airplanes, the sailors nevertheless shook their fists at them and made obscene gestures in their direction.

While the men on the British ships waited in a state of disquiet and impatience for the result of Holland's negotiations, the Cabinet waited with even greater expectancy back in England. British troops had seized various French vessels in British ports that morning, in one case leading to three deaths (two British and one French). With this success fresh in the minds, the statesmen quickly grew irritable at Somerville's seemingly dilatory approach. Truculent messages began reaching *Hood* and *Ark Royal* demanding an explanation for why the French had not yet surrendered their ships.

As afternoon came, the French and British alike took their lunch mess. On board the *Strasbourg,* the young officers convened a conference of their own over the meal, one attended by an unexpected guest: Dufay. Dufay, who ordinarily ate with his crew on board the *Bretagne*, apprised the others of the negotiations. Predictably, the fiery officers responded with outrage at the behavior of the British. One of them, the youthful Lieutenant Jean Boutron, launched into a brief tirade: "But we are not beaten. Do you feel beaten, with our *Bretagne* intact? The *Provence* alongside, is she beaten? And the *Dunkerque* and *Strasbourg* – brand flaming new and full of guns and shells – are they beaten? And the rest of the Navy? In any case, I'm not beaten. And I'm not going along with this." (Smith, 2009, 61).

At the same time, the Admiralty staff onshore, attempting to strengthen Gensoul's position, broadcast messages directly to him stating that they would dispatch all available fleet elements, amounting to 50 ships plus submarines, to his aid. They did not encode these messages because they wanted the British to intercept and read these communications, thus indirectly but clearly threatening the annihilation of Force H if it engaged in hostilities.

The British did receive the messages but were unfazed. Somerville had his orders, and he would follow them as he must. Furthermore, the British were certain the action at Mers-le-Kebir would be over before any serious relief fleet could muster, assuming that it even existed in the first place.

At around 1:30 in the afternoon, the French lookouts raised a fresh alarm. Binoculars trained on the mouth of the harbor revealed that five Swordfish biplanes from *Ark Royal* had arrived. Each of the biplanes swooped low, and the observers readily distinguished the shapes of large magnetic sea mines being dropped into the water at the harbor entrance. Somerville had ordered the mining of Mers-el-Kebir's entrance an hour and a half before the deadline expired at 3:00 to prevent the ships from escaping in the meantime. The mines came from a type which sank to the bottom and carried a delayed fuse. The magnetic signature of a ship's prow would activate the fuse, which would then detonate shortly afterward, hopefully destroying the engine room and crippling the ship immediately. Somerville might well have hoped that this display would prompt Gensoul to see the light, and that the British threat of violence was not merely a bluff.

At 2:40 p.m., just 20 minutes before the deadline marking the time the British would attack, Gensoul sent a fresh message to Somerville. The French admiral said that he would see "Hooky"

Holland in person, rather than through his intermediary Dufay. Somerville agreed, despite suspecting that the French merely sought to play him for time. Nevertheless, seeing Holland directly might represent a breakthrough, so he extended the deadline to 5:30 p.m. and ordered Holland to board as soon as possible.

This proved somewhat difficult because the HMS *Foxhound,* expecting fighting to break out, had withdrawn 7.5 miles from the entrance to Mers-el-Kebir harbor. Nevertheless, in the blazing heat of the afternoon, Holland and his immediate entourage clambered down the furnace-like metal side of the warship into their motorboat and set out for the mouth of the harbor once again. The motorboat launched at around 3:00 p.m., and it required a full hour to reach Mers-el-Kebir and bring the boat into the harbor.

By this point, Churchill and his inner war cabinet, despite efforts by other ministers to calm them, had worked themselves into a passion over Somerville's delays. A series of vague but menacing signals began arriving at *Hood's* signals room once again, including one stating that if Somerville did not act he could expect reinforcements. In essence, the government was hinting that ships would be sent with a replacement commander, effectively threatening to cashier him.

Once in the harbor, Holland transferred onto the admiral's barge, once again under the command of Lieutenant Dufay, and traveled the rest of the way to the *Dunkerque.* At long last, Holland found himself piped over the side and escorted to Gensoul's cabin. There, Gensoul, his Chief of Staff, and Dufay conferred with Holland and his aide, Lieutenant Commander Davies. Boiling hot, the cabin had no true ventilation and provided an extremely uncomfortable venue for a discussion destined to last for almost 90 minutes. Gensoul, who had been in the open air on the bridge for most of the day, sweltered in his dress uniform. Holland also immediately noticed that the French admiral showed every sign of barely suppressed fury at the situation.

The fury did not remain suppressed for long. Gensoul began coldly but within moments started bellowing in rage, denouncing British actions and stating that attacking the neutral French fleet could only be construed as an act of war. Holland had expected this type of outburst; in fact, he fully understood it was quite natural for a powerful commander who had been frustrated by threats and demands for most of the day to vent his feelings in the most forceful manner possible. Accordingly, he listened without allowing the words to disturb him.

However, Gensoul's final words did take him aback for a moment. The French admiral pointed out that the three clauses which would have the ships sail elsewhere (to England, the West Indies, etc.) could not be carried out since the British had already mined the harbor entrance, leaving him only the alternatives of scuttling or fighting. He then asserted once more that he would not let the Germans or Italians take the ships.

Holland recovered quickly and, bypassing the somewhat cogent issue of the minelaying, brought up the problem of Axis forces seizing the ships. "Although we trusted his word and the similar promises given by Admiral Ollive de Laborde and Esteva that they would do everything possible to prevent their ships falling into enemy hands, we could not trust the Germans or the Italians who would by treachery do all they could to achieve this end. Admiral Gensoul, however, would not listen to this argument and said he was convinced that steps taken were adequate to sink his ships whatever happened. I pointed out that by sinking his ships, he would anyway be breaking the terms of the Armistice, and by his own action. Should he accept any one of the terms we had offered to him that morning, he would be acting under "Force majeur" and the blame for any action taken would rest on us. To this, he replied that, so long as Germany and Italy abided by the Armistice terms, and allowed the French Fleet to remain with reduced crews, flying the French flag in a French Metropolitan or Colonial port, he should do the same, and not until Germany or Italy had broken their promises would he break the terms laid down, and that these were his orders signed by Admiral Darlan." (War Diaries, 1940, 4-5, Web).

The circular argument continued on and on until 5:15, when Somerville signaled *Dunkerque* that if Gensoul did not accept the terms in the next 15 minutes, the British would sink his ships. At this point, Gensoul, now friendly to Holland, shook his hand, thanked him for his negotiating services, and gave him a copy of his orders from Darlan, which disallowed handing over the vessels to any other party – British, German, Italian, etc. – up to and including scuttling them if no alternative existed to prevent their capture.

Holland hurried up on deck, not knowing how punctually Somerville's bombardment would begin. The French officers saluted him as he clambered over the side into the barge and returned to his motorboat, and the British officer could not restrain tears from trickling down his face. He later reported being one mile from the harbor entrance when the first British shell howled over the ocean surface to plunge into a French ship, thus beginning the brief and bloody action of Mers-el-Kebir.

The Attack

At 5:54 p.m., Somerville issued the single-word command to launch the attack over the radio to Force H: "Anvil." At the same time, the signalers raised the red and white flags, which meant "open fire," to the top of *Hood's* signaling mast. Immediately, the battleship's guns sent their first salvo towards the anchored French ships with a deafening, thunderous boom that quivered through the entire vessel.

At this point, the French flotilla in Mers-el-Kebir consisted of four battleships – *Dunkerque, Strasbourg, Bretagne,* and *Provence* - a seaplane tender, *Commandant Teste*, and six destroyers, *Mogador, Volta, Terrible, Kersaint, Lynx,* and *Tigre.* The British naturally chose the battleships as priority targets due to their higher threat level.

To allow the ships a better chance to escape the harbor without falling victim to the British magnetic mines dropped by aircraft earlier in the day, French patrol boats had sailed out to the torpedo net during Holland's prolonged interview with Gensoul. The men aboard riddled the buoys supporting the net with machine gun fire until the buoys and the steel net they supported sank to the bottom of the harbor. This increased the usable channel width, which might hopefully allow the warships to slip past the mines.

As soon as the first gunfire flashes appeared out to sea in the gathering dusk, Gensoul's ship signaled with flags for the ships to make for the open sea. The destroyers, faster and more maneuverable, headed for the entrance first, both to allow their speedy escape and to clear the harbor for the larger, more cumbersome vessels.

The first British shells plowed into the sea beyond the jetty, sending white fountains of spray leaping high into the air. This gave observers on the ships the ranging information they needed to correct their aim. The second salvo struck the jetty itself. *Strasbourg* had moved clear of the jetty, but a crew of French sailors were still laboring to cast off *Dunkerque*'s moorings at the moment the shells arrived. A 15-inch shell weighing 2,000 pounds slammed directly into the middle of the men and exploded, transforming them instantly into a shower of severed heads and limbs, shredded flesh and bone, and intestines pattering down into the water and the *Dunkerque*'s decks.

180 men died on board the *Dunkerque* during this second salvo. Shells plunged into the ship's engine room, blowing dozens of men apart instantly. Steam exploded from the ruptured boilers, boiling some men alive in seconds. Others, horribly scalded, staggered out of the steam only to be drenched in a sudden tidal wave of burning oil, where they burned to death. Yet more reached the emergency hatches, which no longer worked automatically due to loss of power and had to be forced slowly open using backup pumps.

One of the *Dunkerque*'s engines still worked, and several brave men remained at their post in the midst of the inferno, keeping it functioning as the flagship finally lurched away from the jetty.

Massive British shells continued to scream in from the sea at a range of 17,600 yards and smash into the French vessels. The *Bretagne* began to take serious hits as well. Lieutenant Jean Boutron, who earlier expressed his refusal to be beaten, now occupied his fire control turret at the moment that British shells slammed into the vessel and set its oil reserves alight. Fire completely engulfed the ship and spread across the harbor around it within 7 minutes. Two minutes later, the ship rolled over with a tremendous roar as seawater flooding in struck the boilers and erupted into explosive steam. In short order, the vessel capsized entirely and sank. Boutron survived only because he had stepped out of his turret in an effort to get a better view, a frame of reference for his rangefinding. At the moment he stepped out, the deck tilted under him as the *Bretagne*'s colossal mass rolled over faster and faster. The motion flung Boutron into the oil-filled water, where he sank but eventually surfaced.

An ordinary French sailor on board the *Bretagne,* Andre Jaffe, also left an account of the battleship's sinking: "A shell exploded underneath, where there were munitions and a fuel store. I saw a friend who'd had his head blown off. His blood dripped off me. I wanted to be sick. The water was black with oil that was smoking and bubbling, like a chip pan, and men were struggling and screaming in it. But I had to jump in. I fell into that oil and I let myself sink, sink, sink. I was so burned." (Craig, 2010, Web).

1,079 men died on the *Bretagne,* while only 180 survived. Boutron lived because a doctor whom he knew pulled him from the oily water and managed to beat and push on his chest and stomach enough for him to cough and vomit out the huge amount of oil he had swallowed.

A picture of the *Bretagne* on fire

Shells continued to strike the *Dunkerque* in the meantime, inflicting more damage and knocking out much of its remaining power. With the ship almost completely crippled, it steered towards the beach under the shadow of Fort Santon, whose massive walls would at least partially shelter it from the incoming shells. In all, 210 officers and men perished aboard the *Dunkerque,* the vast majority in the first few seconds of the attack.

Illustrating once again the randomness of battle, shells smashed destructively into the *Provence,* moored alongside the *Dunkerque* when the action began. Though the ship's structure suffered extreme damage, only three men in total died on board the battleship, preserved from slaughter only by the vagaries of fate.

The *Strasbourg* fared best of all. The large, powerful ship got underway immediately when the shell splashes erupted outside the jetty, and the salvo aimed at it struck an empty berth instead. Picking up speed, the steel colossus churned forward through the black veils of smoke, its prow pushing through floating wreckage, burning oil, and the mangled corpses of men. As the Frenchmen on the other ships spotted the huge vessel rushing steadily out of the harbor mouth, thousands of voices began to cheer enthusiastically at this escape.

By this point, the smoke rising from the stricken ships had created an almost total smokescreen over Mers-el-Kebir. The British failed to spot the *Strasbourg* in the murk as it ran out to sea and slipped past their distant blockade. *Mogador*, one of the destroyers, attempted the same but took a hit in the stern, which exploded its entire arsenal of depth charges simultaneously and chopped off the rear end of the ship. The destroyer's internal watertight compartments kept it from sinking, and another ship later towed it to the beach. 38 men died on board, but 200 survived.

The other five destroyers also made good their escape, forming up on *Strasbourg* as an escort. Fire from the other French ships and land fortifications splashed around the British ships, providing additional distraction, though none scored a hit despite dozens of shells hurled back at the British vessels. This led to the later French legend that Gensoul's men had fired into the air in order to provide the appearance of resistance, but in a way that would result in no casualties.

Somerville now signaled Gensoul that he would open fire again if the French did not accept the terms. Gensoul hoisted a square flag – a sign of capitulation pursuant to the terms handed to him by the British earlier in the day – and signaled back that he would comply with the British demands. In fact, he had no intention of doing so, but he was trying to buy time for his men.

Simultaneously, far away on the continent, the French diffidently approached Otto von Stülpnagel and his Armistice Commission in Wiesbaden. They explained the actions taken by Gensoul, which represented a violation of multiple articles of the Armistice, and asked for a special exemption due to the British attack. Somewhat to their surprise, von Stülpnagel, still eager to take a conciliatory line to the French, indicated his favorable inclination to the idea. He, in turn, contacted Hitler, and the Fuhrer readily agreed to the suspension for the duration of the emergency, effectively restoring complete freedom of action to the Vichy fleet until the matter could be resolved. Gensoul's actions would not bring the wrath of the Germans down on his country, and he basically now had a free hand to proceed as he thought best.

Otto von Stülpnagel

Somerville and his leading officers didn't believe the first scouting aircraft report of the *Strasbourg* steaming away east. However, a second airplane with the same news arrived shortly thereafter, and now the British admiral realized that multiple vessels had slipped out of the net he believed inescapable. He accordingly passed word to "Nutty" Wells of the *Ark Royal* to send his aircraft to bomb the escaping battleship and destroyers.

A trio of Blackburn Skua fighters took off to escort the six bomb-equipped Swordfish sent to harry the fleeing French. With nightfall coming on, the British did not have long to locate their quarry, but the skilled pilots found the *Strasbourg* and made an attack run to drop their 250 pound bombs. A storm of flak fire rose to greet them, filling the sky with the bursting dark clusters of shrapnel. One Skua suddenly flamed and banked into the sea, killing the pilot.

The Swordfish dropped their bombs and skimmed away, clinging close to the surface of the water in an effort to avoid being hit. Nevertheless, flak shell fragments shredded two of the bombers, which crashed into the sea at different points on the return flight. HMS *Wrestler* managed to save both crews. In all, the bombing run did no damage whatsoever to the French.

A second squadron sent out under Captain G.B. Hodgkinson found the *Strasbourg* and dropped six torpedoes into the water, aimed at the huge French ship. The attack occurred shortly after sunset and, flying in low, the six Swordfish attracted only desultory machine gun fire. The aircraft achieved two hits but neither torpedo inflicted much damage, and the *Strasbourg* sailed on into the shelter of the night.

During the night, the French in Mers-el-Kebir worked to retrieve their dead and rescue survivors still floating in the harbor. The seaplane tender *Commandant Teste* carried out most of the rescue operations after being miraculously unharmed during the bombardment. Saving the men in the oily water proved a nightmarish task, however. Coated in a thick layer of oil, they slithered out of the rescuers' grasp time and time again. Some drowned within arm's reach of safety because they were too slippery to be pulled from the water or grip lines or the sides of boats.

Meanwhile, now out at sea, *Strasbourg* and the destroyers swung around Sardinia and made for Toulon harbor. The *Ark Royal* prepared its aircraft through the night for a bombing attack on the ships remaining in Mers-el-Kebir.

When morning dawned, thick fog lay over the sea, harbor, and land, blanking out all targets. Somerville called off the air raid due to zero visibility, and instead Force H steamed back to Gibraltar to report, refuel, and resupply with ammunition. At this point, with war between Britain and Vichy France hanging in the balance, the submarine HMS *Pandora's* skipper, Lieutenant Commander JW Linton, nearly opened a veritable Pandora's Box when he interpreted "Operation Catapult" as meaning open season on all French shipping.

As his Admiralty report recounted:

> "1358 hours – Sighted 'what is thought to be' a La Galissioniere class light cruiser. Enemy course was 090°, speed 17 knots, range 4 nautical miles.
>
> 1407 hours – Fired four torpedoes from 3800 yards. Two or three hits were obtained. The target stopped and was heavily on fire.
>
> 1522 hours – The target was seen to sink, stern first. This was followed by a extremely heavy explosion, possibly her after magazines blowing up." (Linton, 1940, Web).

In fact, Linton had just torpedoed a French Bougainville-class colonial sloop, the *Rigault de Genouilly*, under the command of Captain Louis Frossard. The lightly armed sloop, designed for patrolling off French colonial possessions, sank rapidly, drowning 12 of its 177 man crew. A second sloop and three French aircraft attempted to depth charge *Pandora*, while two fishing boats rescued Frossard's surviving crew.

The British apologized profusely to the French for this error, but another disaster had begun to brew, this time due to an error by the French Admiralty. Admiral Darlan issued an order making Admiral Jean-Pierre Esteva Commander-in-Chief of the French Atlantic Fleet. Esteva, in turn, immediately sent out a wireless message of encouragement claiming that the *Dunkerque* – actually crippled and beached – had suffered only trivial damage and would be ready for action again in days.

When the British intercepted this message, they immediately decided to return to Mers-el-Kebir to finish the job. Somerville had intended to leave the harbor be, but Esteva's message – totally inaccurate as it was – gave him the impression that his job remained undone. The British set sail on the night of July 5-6, returning to the wreckage-strewn desolation of Mers-el-Kebir.

At dawn on the 6th, flights of Swordfish escorted by Skuas suddenly burst out of the summer haze over the lazily-undulating Algerian sea. The French, utterly stunned, found the *Dunkerque*'s mangled hulk being pounded with a fresh hail of bombs. One of the men who witnessed the attack described the huge ship's condition afterward as "hallucinatory."

Even worse, the succeeding waves of planes spotted the trawler Terra Neuve anchored alongside the *Dunkerque*, busily taking men off the wreck of the flagship. Mistaking it for a full-sized warship (it had been converted to an anti-submarine patrol craft with the addition of depth charges, but it did not represent part of the force Somerville had orders to sink), they launched their torpedoes into it. Unarmored, the Terra Neuve shattered upon impact, and its store of depth charges erupted in a colossal explosion. The blast caused a vast black fountain of oil-filled water to spurt up into the air, filled with wreckage and human body parts. This ghastly mixture then fell like an inky rain over the ship, the water nearby, and the shore, seeming to gush down endlessly out of the sky. The damage had torn the trawler's hull wide open. With a deep bubbling sound, it slipped under the black water, carrying dead, dying, and wounded men with it.

For the French, the final toll for the action at Mers-el-Kebir amounted to 1,297 officers and men killed and 351 wounded. The French buried their dead in Oran cemetery, where they would lie undisturbed until massive vandalism in 2006 destroyed most of their memorials. Admiral Gensoul attended the ceremony, providing something of an epitaph for his slain compatriots when he said, "If there is a stain on the flag, it is certainly not on ours."

The Aftermath of Mers-el-Kebir

Admiral Somerville felt nothing but relief at the end of Operation Catapult. Immediately after the action, back in Gibraltar, he wrote a letter to his wife. Part of it read, "Afraid I shall get a colossal raspberry from the Admiralty for letting the battlecruiser escape. In fact, I shouldn't be surprised if I was relieved forthwith. I don't mind because it was an absolutely bloody business to shoot up those Frenchmen who showed the greatest gallantry. The truth is my heart wasn't in it and you're not allowed a heart in wartime." (Heckstall-Smith, 1963, 104).

For his part, Admiral Darlan responded to the attack with cold, concentrated fury. He issued an order that Vichy ships should attack British ships wherever they encountered them, a command which, if carried out, would have led to war between the two nations. Additionally, he contacted the Italian Navy and sounded them out on the topic of a joint operation to attack and destroy the British task force then located at Alexandria, Egypt.

Marshal Petain intervened personally the following day, countermanding Darlan's attack order and preventing the eruption of war between Vichy France and England. This also ended Darlan's plan of joining with the Italians for a revenge attack on Alexandria, which, though perhaps understandable, would have committed Vichy France to the Axis side, a move Petain was not prepared to make.

Following the attack at Mers-el-Kebir, anger swept over France. Volunteers for the Free French fell off to a fraction of what they had been immediately before the operation, remaining at a greatly reduced level for some time. Even de Gaulle protested the action, though his precarious position as a guest of the British compelled him to limit his outrage.

The Germans, led by propaganda minister Joseph Goebbels, pounced on the attack as a golden opportunity to whip up French resentment against Britain to fresh heights. Goebbels briefed his men at the propaganda ministry on the opportunity he saw in the action at Mers-el-Kebir, which, like the British, he referred to as "Oran." "The British Navy's attack on the French Fleet at Oran is to be used for a detailed exposition of how Britain first dragged France into the war, how she then let France make the main preparations, […] how French divisions bled themselves white while the British carried out a 'withdrawal without losses' policy, […] and how, to top it all, they were now attacking the French ships – all 'in France's interest.' Here Britain has really revealed herself without her mask." (Boelcke, 1970, 63).

The French scarcely needed German encouragement to respond to Operation Catapult with outrage. For some time, Frenchmen at all levels of society, including politicians, military men, and ordinary citizens, lobbied their government to fully join the Axis so that they could render direct military aid against England. Marshal Petain, the head of the Vichy government, used all his influence, popularity, and authority as a decorated war hero to prevent this juncture between Vichy France and the Third Reich. He succeeded in averting the impulses of his countrymen, thereby rendering a considerable service to the Free French and British, who would later imprison him for life despite calls for clemency by President Harry Truman.

Churchill roused further French fury a month later when he made one of his famous political speeches. While openly weeping, he declared Operation Catapult a "melancholy action" and praised the courage of both the British and French seamen as though it had been a natural disaster rather than a plan devised mostly by him and carried out doggedly over the objections of his admirals. Though the French and some of the British thought it exceedingly hypocritical, it drew a thunderous ovation from the politicians in the House of Commons.

Ironically, Operation Catapult placed the French fleet in much greater danger of falling into German hands than existed before the British attack. Vichy France had intended to keep their ships in African ports, utterly inaccessible to the Wehrmacht and nearly as safe from the weak surface forces of the Kriegsmarine. This plan protected France's overseas holdings while eliminating the hazard of German fleet confiscation. However, the African ports left the ships vulnerable to Royal Navy aggression. Rather than see their vessels sunk uselessly and their sailors killed by the thousand, the Vichy navy withdrew most of their warships to French ports, concentrating the majority at Toulon. While this measure protected the ships from the English, it made them easily accessible to seizure by German land troops, precisely the outcome Churchill and his cabinet claimed Operation Catapult would avert.

For nearly two years, the Germans observed the terms of the Armistice for the most part, to the surprise of the French. However, in November 1942, when the French forces in North Africa rapidly changed sides after the Allies landed to the west, Hitler decided to take the remainder of France, principally in order to secure the Mediterranean coast with German divisions but also to settle the fate of the ships at Toulon. Accordingly, the Wehrmacht and Waffen SS launched Case Anton, a sudden offensive into Vichy French territory that conquered the quasi-independent nation and added it to the Third Reich as a German imperial possession.

With characteristic speed and energy, German units executed Operation Lila to commandeer the large collection of French naval ships and submarines at Toulon. The 7th Panzer Division, supplemented by other units including elite motorcycle battalions from the 2nd SS Panzer Division *Das Reich*, sped south and nearly succeeded in capturing the Vichy fleet on November 27, 1942. However, the French Rear Admiral Dornon and Admiral Laborde, with great presence of mind and professionalism, managed to give the order to scuttle the ships.

The French used every trick available to them to delay German boarding, and for their part, the Wehrmacht and Waffen SS men showed great reluctance to use force against the French sailors, carrying on the conciliatory approach the Germans had shown towards handling the Vichy fleet from the start and preferring attempts at negotiation and persuasion.

Ultimately, the French managed to set off most of their scuttling charges, destroying 77 vessels and proving in the most emphatic manner possible that Admiral Darlan had indeed told Churchill the truth when he vowed the Vichy government would use any means necessary to keep the ships out of German hands.

Online Resources

Other World War II titles by Charles River Editors

Other titles about Operation Catapult on Amazon

Bibliography

Auphan, Rear Admiral Paul, Jacques Mordal, and Captain ACJ Sabalot, USN   (translator). The French Navy in World War II. Annapolis, 2016.

Callil, Carmen. Bad Faith: A Forgotten History of Family, Fatherland and Vichy France. New

York, 2006.

Christofferson, Michael, and Thomas Christofferson. France During World War II: From Defeat to Liberation. New York, 2006.

Craig, Phil. "Mass murder or a stroke of genius that saved Britain? As closer ties with France are planned, the 'betrayal' they still can't forgive." DailyMail.com. 5 February 2010, Web. http://www.dailymail.co.uk/news/article-1248615/Mass-murder-stroke-genius-saved-Britain-As-closer-ties-France-planned-betrayal-forgive.html

Grainger, John D. Traditional Enemies: Britain's War With Vichy France, 1940-1942. Barnsley, 2013.

Griffiths, Richard. Marshal Petain. London, 2011.

Heckstall-Smith, Anthony. The Fleet that Faced Both Ways. London, 1963.

Hellman, John. The Knight-Monks of Vichy France: Uriage, 1940-45. Quebec City, 1993.

Jackson, Julian. France: The Dark Years, 1940-1944. Oxford, 2001.

Jones, Howard. The Crucible of Power: A History of American Foreign Relations from 1897. Plymouth, 2008.

Lacouture, Jean. De Gaulle: The Rebel 1890–1944. London, 1991.

Linton, JW. Report ADM 199/283. The National Archives, Kew. 1940. Web.

https://uboat.net/allies/warships/ship/3404.html

Lormier, Dominique. Mers El-Kebir Juillet 1940 (Documents, Actualités, Société). Paris, 2007.

Pearson, Christopher. Scarred Landscapes: War and Nature in Vichy France. London, 2008.

Roskill, Stephen. Churchill and the Admirals. Barnsley, 2004.

Smith, Colin. England's Last War Against France: Fighting Vichy 1940-1942. London, 2010.

Sumner, Ian and Francois Vauvillier. The French Army 1939-45 (I): The Army of 1930-40 & Vichy France. Oxford, 1998.

Sweets, John F. Choices in Vichy France: The French under Nazi Occupation. Oxford, 1994.

Tute, Warren. *The Deadly Stroke.* Barnsley, 2007.

War Diaries, Force H. *Narrative of Events on July 3rd, 1940.* ADM 199/391. The National Archives, Kew. 1940. Web. http://www.admirals.org.uk/records/adm/adm199/adm199-391_32-53.php

Free Books by Charles River Editors

We have brand new titles available for free most days of the week. To see which of our titles are currently free, click on this link.

Discounted Books by Charles River Editors

We have titles at a discount price of just 99 cents everyday. To see which of our titles are currently 99 cents, click on this link.

CPSIA information can be obtained
at www.ICGtesting.com
Printed in the USA
BVHW042119090719
553037BV00016B/210/P

9 781986 387804